THE
KOBE
WAY

THE KOBE WAY

THE ICONIC MOMENTS AND MANEUVERS
THAT MADE HIM A LEGEND

BRIAN BOONE • ILLUSTRATED BY **BRIT SIGH**

CASTLE POINT BOOKS
NEW YORK

"GREAT THINGS COME FROM HARD WORK AND PERSEVERANCE.

NO EXCUSES."

CONTENTS

THE *KOBE* WAY

Anybody at least a little familiar with the sport can agree that Kobe Bryant is among the absolute best to ever play basketball. But unlike other stars considered the greatest of all time—Michael Jordan, LeBron James, Magic Johnson—Kobe Bryant didn't set many records. He ranked #4 on the all-time scoring list, #13 in most three-pointers made, #15 in games played, and #33 in assists. But what Kobe did really well was win games, which he did a lot. Over twenty seasons, Kobe's teams amassed a record of 836 wins and 510 losses, along with five NBA championships. Individual stats reflect an individual's greatness, but the numbers of games and titles won better reflect the widespread and influential impact of Kobe Bryant.

He didn't just succeed on the court. Instead, he actively sought to improve his skills and those of his teammates, inspiring himself and others to achieve greatness in basketball and other endeavors. Kobe possessed what he called the "Mamba Mentality." Like a deadly snake, he focused on his prey—transcendent greatness—and doggedly pursued it with everything he had. Kobe never quit, never gave up, and never stopped trying to improve.

Here are twenty-five stories—with important and profound lessons—about the legendary, never-to-be-forgotten Kobe Bryant, tales of triumph and achievement that truly demonstrate *The Kobe Way*.

CHAPTER 1
THE MOVE

Kobe Bryant just *loved* basketball, and his personality and playing style were well suited to the game, which is all about individual games, plays, and moments. Kobe relentlessly executed plays every single time he hit the court for the Los Angeles Lakers in his twenty-year career. Highly competitive and intensely prepared, he gave his all to try to score the bucket or win the game, be it a regular season game or an important playoffs contest.

Kobe was a player who came through in the clutch for his teammates. He frequently became a late-game hero, providing unexpected, exhilarating, and almost impossible come-from-behind victories. These are some of Kobe's best-ever games and moments.

A SLAM DUNK OF A
FIRST IMPRESSION

Kobe Bryant was among the very top and most elite of all NBA players for nearly the entirety of his twenty-year career, and he was rightfully selected for the NBA All-Star Game rosters eighteen times, the second-highest selected in league history (trailing only fellow Los Angeles Lakers great, Kareem Abdul-Jabbar). On those eighteen squads, Bryant was named a starter fourteen times, and on his first in 1998, he became the youngest All-Star starter ever at just nineteen years old. He'd eventually be named the All-Star Game MVP four times. But Bryant's first appearance at NBA All-Star Weekend came in February 1997, during his rookie season. He wasn't on the Western Conference All-Star roster—he was a backup point guard for the Lakers that first year, averaging a meager 7.6 points.

But Kobe embraced the moment and showed the other All-Stars that he belonged in their company, participating in (and dominating) the annual league-wide Slam Dunk Contest. After Chris Carr and Darvin Ham delivered tricky 360-degree dunks, Kobe swaggered out onto the court and did a floating up-and-under dunk, splitting his legs. That thunderous dunk made Kobe a known entity—as did his thirty-one points in the rookie game.

"THE MOST
IMPORTANT THING
IS YOU MUST PUT
EVERYBODY ON NOTICE
THAT YOU'RE HERE
AND YOU ARE FOR REAL."

★ FACT ★

Kobe Bryant is the
SECOND-HIGHEST
overall scorer in All-Star Game
history. In 2020, the game's MVP
trophy was named in his honor.

SETTING THE SUNS

The Los Angeles Lakers finished the 2005–2006 regular season with a 45–37 record, squeaking into the playoffs as the Western Conference's seventh seed (out of eight teams), earning a first-round matchup with the #2-ranked, division-winning, and heavily favored Phoenix Suns.

Kobe Bryant led both teams in scoring in Games 1 and 2, won by the Suns and Lakers, respectively, setting up a Game 3 on which the series' momentum would hinge. And with just 7.9 seconds left in the game, it looked like the Suns would close out the win, leading 90 to 88. Starting up after a timeout, Phoenix's Boris Diaw inbounded the ball to that season's MVP, Steve Nash, only for the Lakers' Smush Parker to immediately knock it away and steal it. Both teams zoomed to the Lakers' basket, with Parker tossing the ball to Devean George, who threw it to Kobe, by far the first member of his squad to reach the hoop. Guarded by four Suns defenders around the hoop, Kobe avoided all comers (and a block attempt by Diaw) to lay in the ball and tie the game as the game clock expired. Kobe's successful buzzer-beating layup sent the game into overtime, which the Lakers won, a crucial victory in a series they'd also capture—one of only five times a #7 seed beat a #2 seed.

★ FACT ★

Kobe Bryant sits at **#21** on the list of most made three-pointers of all time, with 1,827. But in 2003, he set a record for most threes made in a single game: **11**.

"I DON'T WANT
TO BE THE NEXT
MICHAEL JORDAN.
I ONLY WANT TO
BE KOBE BRYANT."

EIGHTY-ONE

The record for most points scored by one player in an NBA game is one hundred, set by Wilt Chamberlain in 1962. But basketball was played very differently in those days, with more offense, less defense, and different rules. In the years since, only two other players had scored more than seventy, but then Kobe Bryant set the modern-day record for most points in an NBA game.

Kobe's 2005–2006 season was already among his best yet—he'd go on to win that year's scoring title. On January 22, 2006, a home game for the Los Angeles Lakers against the Toronto Raptors began with Kobe scoring well. In the first half, he scored twenty-six points, with the Lakers trailing 63 to 49. In the third quarter, Kobe exploded and almost couldn't miss. He made 73 percent of the shots he took, putting the Lakers up by six points. Kobe had scored fifty-three points, a monumental night for any NBA player, and he'd only played in three quarters. After landing twenty-seven points in the third quarter, he scored even more in the fourth quarter, amassing another twenty-eight points. That made for a grand total of eighty-one points, a personal best for Kobe and every other NBA player in more than forty years, as well as a win for his Lakers.

"WE CAN ALWAYS
KIND OF BE AVERAGE
AND DO WHAT'S NORMAL.
I'M NOT IN THIS
TO DO WHAT'S NORMAL."

THE WILD THREE

With the winner going to the NBA Finals, the 2009 Western Conference Finals pitted the top two seeds, the Los Angeles Lakers and Denver Nuggets, against each other, each led by a legend—veteran Kobe Bryant and rising star Carmelo Anthony. Kobe's forty points led the Lakers to a Game 1 win, while his thirty-two points wasn't enough to get past Anthony and the Nuggets in Game 2. With a little over a minute left in the pivotal Game 3 of the series, Denver led 95 to 93.

The Lakers got the ball and left it to point guard and team leader Kobe Bryant to get the win. With ten seconds remaining on the shot clock, he ran all around the key, pursued doggedly by his defender, the tough and tenacious J.R. Smith, with Anthony also looking to prevent Kobe from scoring. Well back from the three-point line and almost out of bounds, and with Smith standing just inches in front of him with his arms in his face, Kobe faded back and attempted a three-point shot. He was barely able to get it off in time, but it went in—nothing but net. The Lakers won the game and would go on to win the series with two blowout victories (in which Kobe Bryant led his team in scoring).

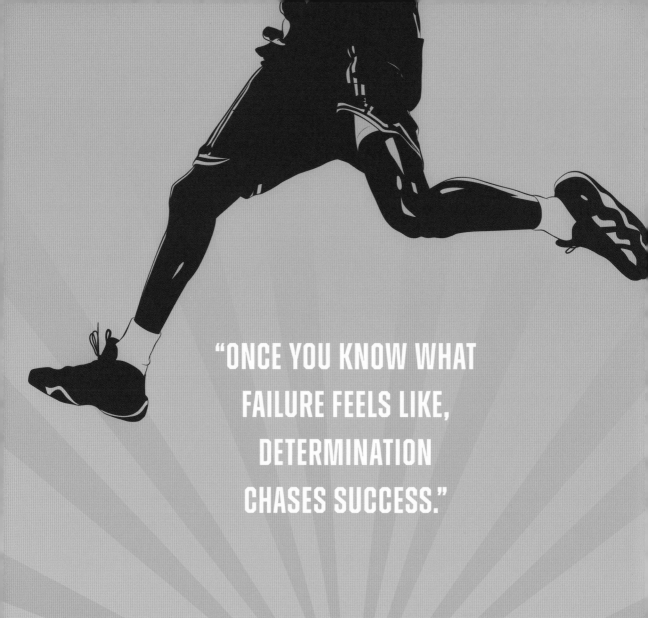

"ONCE YOU KNOW WHAT FAILURE FEELS LIKE, DETERMINATION CHASES SUCCESS."

KOBE!

Kobe Bryant is the Los Angeles Lakers' **ALL-TIME LEADER** in games played, minutes played, points scored, and shots both attempted and made.

THAT'S *SO* MAMBA

Kobe Bryant is 1 OF ONLY 6 PLAYERS *in* NBA HISTORY TO BE NAMED AN NBA *Finals* MVP IN BACK-TO-BACK YEARS.

KOBE *BEING* KOBE

Kobe played in 6 decisive seventh games—and he **WON 4 OF THEM,** 3 of which sealed NBA Finals victories.

GO, KOBE, GO!

Kobe is **1** of only **5** Los Angeles Lakers to win **5 championships,** joining Michael Cooper, Derek Fisher, Magic Johnson, and Kareem Abdul-Jabbar.

DID *YOU* KNOW?

The most points Kobe ever scored in a game against the Boston Celtics was

43.

He did it in March 2006 and again in January 2007.

THE REMATCH

The rivalry between the Los Angeles Lakers and the Boston Celtics is one of the oldest and most intense in all of sports, with the two franchises squaring off in the NBA Finals a dozen times. In 2008, the Celtics defeated the Lakers four games to two, despite a spectacular performance from Kobe Bryant, who led both teams in scoring, averaging 25.7 points per game. Kobe, by that point a diehard Laker who had only ever played for that team (and only ever would), smarted over the loss and spent the next two seasons angling for a rematch to reclaim the NBA championship from the daunting Celtics. The 2010 NBA Finals would give Kobe a chance for redemption and revenge.

The desire to right the wrongs of the 2008 series fueled Kobe to produce spectacular, game-clinching stats. He averaged 28.5 points per game across the series, and in six of the contests, Kobe was the top scorer on both teams, including a thirty-eight-point performance in Game 5. The series was hard fought, with the Lakers and Celtics trading wins, pushing the Finals to a decisive seventh game. When it came time to give it everything he had, Kobe did, putting up twenty-three points and fifteen rebounds. Final score: Lakers 83 to Celtics 79. Kobe won five NBA championships, but he considered this championship his most personally important.

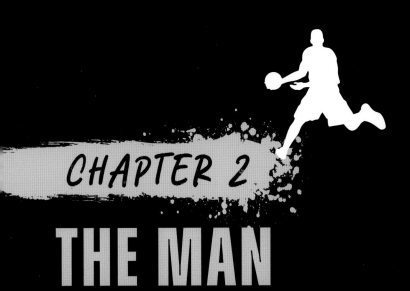

CHAPTER 2

THE MAN

What transforms a regular sports star into a superstar or an all-time great? They don't just have to be good at what they do—they have to be team leaders. A true legend has a drive to win, and they inspire their teammates to try as hard as they do, to have the same goals in mind, and to work toward them. Kobe Bryant was that kind of player, possessing a never-faltering drive to win and the talent to make it happen. Kobe had character and could lead, and he used those skills off and on the court, helping others succeed. Here are five times when Kobe proved he was built differently, that he had something special—a winning and killer instinct—and the leadership to bring out the strengths in others.

TURNING
SILVER TO GOLD

The USA men's basketball team historically dominated the Summer Olympics, particularly after NBA professionals were allowed to compete in 1992. "Dream Team" squads consisting of NBA legends won gold medals in 1992, 1996, and 2000, then surprisingly lost to Argentina in the semifinals of the 2004 Olympics. In 2008, Team USA, led by a redemption- and revenge-seeking team captain Kobe Bryant, cruised to a gold medal, earning itself the nickname "Redeem Team." In the final match for the gold medal, the American national team defeated Spain's national team—led by center Pau Gasol—118 to 107.

Just a few weeks later, Kobe reported to the Los Angeles Lakers' preseason training camp. Toward the end of the previous NBA season, Gasol had joined the Lakers, making him teammates with Kobe, who had just beaten him in the Olympics. Kobe turned any lingering animosity between himself and Gasol into motivation, hanging his treasured gold medal in Gasol's locker. That reminder of coming up short led Gasol to push himself to play harder. At the end of the 2008–2009 season, the Lakers, led by Kobe and Gasol, reached the NBA Finals after two straight years of early playoff exits.

"I ENCOURAGE YOU TO ALWAYS BE CURIOUS, ALWAYS SEEK OUT THINGS YOU LOVE, AND ALWAYS WORK HARD ONCE YOU FIND IT."

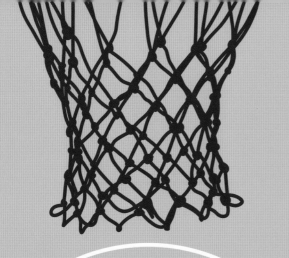

★ FACT ★

In global basketball competition, Kobe played for **5** Team USA squads, winning the 2007 Tournament of the Americas and gold medals at the **2008** and **2012** Olympics— his team's overall win–loss record: **36** and **0**.

LEADING THE LAKERS

Kobe Bryant was often the most prolific offensive force on his Los Angeles Lakers teams, and he frequently took charge in late-game, clutch, must-score moments. Those things, along with his confidence, earned him a reputation as a selfish, self-serving player. But Kobe wasn't so much of a ball hog as he was a team leader who led by example. He was the Lakers' point guard and an unofficial player-coach who relentlessly set up plays for others.

Kobe exemplified this in the 2001 NBA Finals. This series marked the first monumental matchup between their generation's two most important players: Lakers' Kobe Bryant and Philadelphia 76ers' prolifically scoring guard Allen Iverson. Iverson averaged 35.6 points per game. Meanwhile, Kobe stood in the shadows of his teammate Shaquille O'Neal, who averaged thirty-three points per game to Kobe's 24.6. But Kobe led both teams with 5.8 assists per game and contributed eight rebounds per game (a lot for a small-statured guard). After the Sixers took Game 1, Kobe stole the momentum back for his team in Game 2, scoring thirty-one points and amassing eight rebounds, six assists, and two blocks. The tide turned toward the Lakers, thanks to Kobe, and the Lakers won four straight games to clinch an NBA championship.

★ **FACT** ★

Just how clutch was Kobe? He scored **471** total points in overtime periods, setting an **NBA record.**

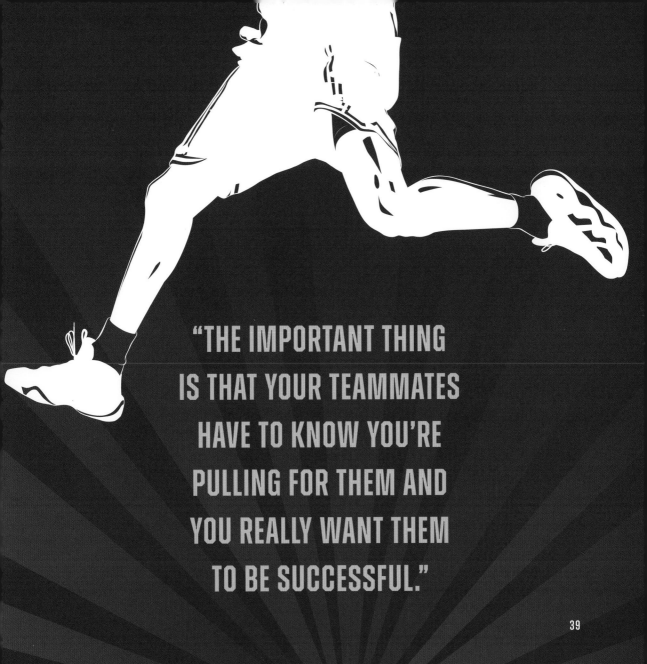

"THE IMPORTANT THING IS THAT YOUR TEAMMATES HAVE TO KNOW YOU'RE PULLING FOR THEM AND YOU REALLY WANT THEM TO BE SUCCESSFUL."

WALKING OFF
THE INJURY

In just his fourth season as a professional basketball player, Kobe Bryant made his first NBA Finals at the end of the 1999–2000 season. That achievement could have been tainted for Kobe, and he could have missed out on all the glory and the chance to compete at the highest level possible. After breezing to a 104 to 87 victory in Game 1 against the Indiana Pacers, the Los Angeles Lakers suffered a potentially catastrophic blow in the first quarter of Game 2 when Kobe tripped on opponent Jalen Rose's foot while coming down from a jump shot. (Rose would later admit that he purposely stuck out his foot to trip up Kobe.)

Kobe was in too much pain to play with a sprained ankle, so he sat out Game 3, which the Pacers won. There was no way Kobe would leave his team in the lurch or give up his chance to play for a title. Thanks to his intensive, recovery-oriented training regimen, Kobe was able to return for Game 4, during which he put on a spectacular performance. He pushed the contest into overtime, and after teammate Shaquille O'Neal fouled out, Kobe took control, scoring the majority of the Lakers' points in overtime. They'd win the NBA championship—Kobe's first—in six games.

"HAVE A GOOD TIME. LIFE IS TOO SHORT TO GET BOGGED DOWN AND BE DISCOURAGED. YOU HAVE TO KEEP MOVING. YOU HAVE TO KEEP GOING. PUT ONE FOOT IN FRONT OF THE OTHER, SMILE, AND JUST KEEP ON ROLLING."

43

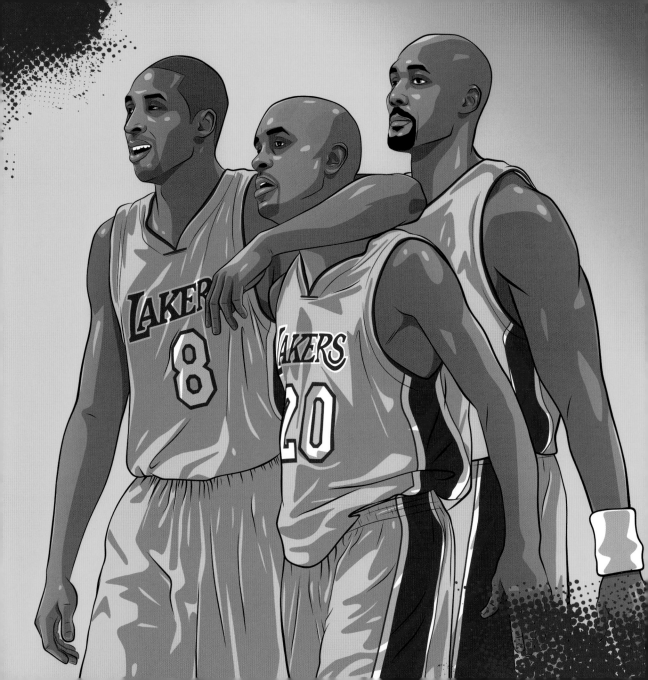

TOP OF THE
SUPER SQUAD

After winning three NBA championships in a row, Kobe Bryant's 2002–2003 Los Angeles Lakers made an early exit in the playoffs, losing to the San Antonio Spurs in the conference finals. Seeking to get back to the top as quickly as possible, the Lakers' management signed Karl Malone and Gary Payton, both nearing the end of their careers and still searching for a championship. Combining Malone and Payton with established Lakers mega-stars Kobe Bryant and Shaquille O'Neal, this roster constituted the first ever "Super Team," and NBA pundits predicted that the Lakers would easily win NBA Finals that year and more games than anyone.

Nevertheless, Kobe didn't relax or consider another title a foregone conclusion. Instead, he worked even harder in training sessions, practice, and research to ensure a Lakers title run. According to Payton, Kobe constantly sought advice from him and Malone, asking them for tips and lessons on how to play better, particularly how to be a better team leader and improve the part of his game he thought needed the most work: defense. Payton, a former NBA Defensive Player of the Year, personally mentored Kobe in that area, and Kobe's defensive skills for the rest of his career improved after that season—a season in which the Lakers reached the NBA Finals.

"I COULD

TELL THAT THE

GAME MEANT MORE

TO ME THAN TO

EVERYBODY ELSE."

★ FACT ★

The 2003–2004 Lakers starting lineup featured 4 players who would be named in the NBA's **75TH ANNIVERSARY TEAM OF GREATS:** Shaquille O'Neal, Karl Malone, Gary Payton, and Kobe Bryant.

47

"*MAMBA* OUT"

At the start of the 2015–2016 NBA season—his twentieth overall—Kobe Bryant announced that he would retire from play at its conclusion, allowing the self-proclaimed "Mamba" to take a victory lap around the league, earning ovations in nearly every NBA city. The Lakers were eliminated from playoff contention early, setting up Kobe's final NBA contest to be the last of the regular season: a home game at Staples Center against the Utah Jazz.

Immediately after the game (which the Lakers won), Kobe was handed a microphone and gave a heartfelt, improvised speech to the fans.

"I grew up a diehard—I mean a diehard Laker fan, diehard. I knew everything about every player that has played here. So to be drafted and then traded to this organization and to spend twenty years here—you can't write something better than this," Kobe said. "It is not about the championships; it is about the down years. We did it the right way; we got our championships. All I can do is thank you guys, thank you guys for all the support, thank you guys for the motivation, thank you guys for the inspiration." Then he expressed gratitude for the fans, his teammates, and his family. "From the bottom of my heart, thank you," Kobe said. "What can I say? Mamba out."

"MAY YOU ALWAYS
REMEMBER TO
ENJOY THE ROAD,
ESPECIALLY WHEN
IT'S A HARD ONE."

THE KOBE WAY

At age 36, Kobe became the oldest player ever to amass a 30-POINT TRIPLE-DOUBLE.

THAT'S SO MAMBA

TO COPE WITH PERSONAL PROBLEMS IN 2003 AND 2004, KOBE CREATED A TOUGH, TENACIOUS, AND UNAPOLOGETIC PERSONA TO ADOPT ON THE COURT, SEPARATING HIS BASKETBALL LIFE FROM HIS OFF-THE-COURT LIFE. HE NAMED THIS SIDE OF HIS PERSONALITY AFTER A DEADLY SNAKE: THE BLACK MAMBA.

KOBE!

Kobe set an NBA record as the oldest player to score 30 POINTS or more in 10 STRAIGHT GAMES.

DID YOU KNOW?

Kobe Bryant's middle name, Bean, is taken from his NBA player father's nickname, Joe "Jellybean" Bryant.

KOBE BEING KOBE

At age 34, Kobe scored MORE THAN 40 all-time leader points and racked up 10 assists in back-to-back games.

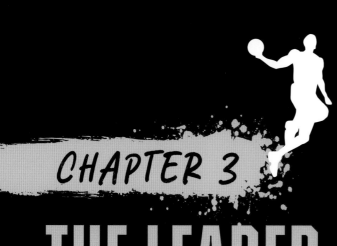

CHAPTER 3

THE LEADER

Basketball was Kobe Bryant's lifelong passion and his area of expertise. When he stopped playing professionally in 2016, he took all the time and energy he'd previously devoted to improving his own game and gave it to younger, up-and-coming basketball stars. Kobe took what he learned about how to be great and passed it on to others to show them how to be great too. He carved out a legacy for himself while also bringing more people into basketball, his favorite thing.

COACHING
KYRIE IRVING

Running the gamut from conversations to individual coaching sessions to lasting mentor-mentee relationships, Kobe Bryant personally and passionately helped many pro basketball players reach their full potential and take their game to new heights. Kobe once stated that among the generation of NBA players that came after him and whom he tutored, he was closest with Kyrie Irving, a fellow point guard, multiple-time All-Star selection, and NBA champion. When Irving helped lead the Cleveland Cavaliers to the 2016 title— after being down three games to one—he video-called Kobe from the locker room celebrations to tell his teacher, "It worked! Your advice worked!"

While spending time together on the U.S. men's basketball team and training together in the offseason (Kobe's final years in the NBA dovetailed with Irving's first ones), many nuts-and-bolts lessons about basketball were shared. But Kobe believed the best advice he ever gave Irving addressed the mental aspect of the game and personal character development. "How do you find an emotional connection with each player?" Kobe recalled discussing with Irving. "Figure out what their fears are and help turn those fears into strengths. And to do that, you have to put time in. I don't mean time in a gym; I mean time listening."

★ FACT ★

Kobe Bryant
claimed to have
NEVER ONCE
lost a game of
one-on-one basketball.

"THE MOST IMPORTANT
THING IS TO TRY AND
INSPIRE PEOPLE SO

COACHING
JAYSON TATUM

Immediately after retiring, Kobe Bryant became an NBA analyst, hosting an ESPN show called *Detail*, where he'd break down footage and offer advice and tips. In a 2018 episode, he covered Boston Celtics rookie Jayson Tatum and was so impressed that he contacted Tatum and offered workouts and coaching sessions during the NBA offseason.

During his playing days and after, Kobe liked to mentor other players, handpicking and pursuing only those men and women who shared his killer instinct for the game and his passion for improvement. Tatum possessed those traits, in part because he'd idolized Kobe as a player since childhood, basing his style on Kobe's on-court moves. But when Kobe took Tatum under his wing, he shared with him the intangibles and extras that Tatum couldn't learn from watching videos, such as footwork, how efficiently Kobe moved his body, and the subtle ways he'd position himself for steals and rebounds. In just the first season after his Kobe coaching sessions began, Tatum's scores, rebounds, assists, and shot attempt averages all skyrocketed.

"IT'S ABOUT HAVING
A FIVE-YEAR PLAN,
A TEN-YEAR PLAN,
AND UNDERSTANDING
HOW TO GET THERE."

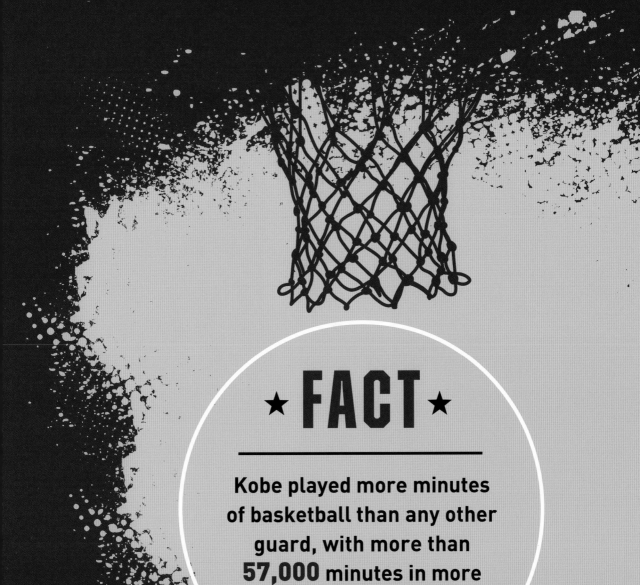

★ FACT ★

Kobe played more minutes
of basketball than any other
guard, with more than
57,000 minutes in more
than **1,500** games.

PUSHING SHAQ

The Los Angeles Lakers made a pronounced effort to assemble a championship-level team in 1996, signing superstar free-agent center Shaquille O'Neal and drafting high school phenom Kobe Bryant. O'Neal, one of the most dominant forces in the NBA at the time, assumed a natural role as a team leader, but as the hyper-competitive and highly skilled Kobe Bryant developed into an offensive dynamo, the duo began to clash. Both players were vying for status as the Lakers' top guy, the one who should have the ball in clutch situations or be the go-to, number-one scoring option.

That mutual resentment and animosity, which turned publicly insulting at times, inspired both Bryant and O'Neal. They became incredibly competitive with one another, each trying to prove himself the superior player. That only helped the Lakers' fortunes, and in the 2000–2001 season, Kobe and Shaq became the highest-scoring duo in NBA history. From 2000 to 2002, Shaq and Kobe's prolific offense and tenacious defense resulted in three consecutive NBA championships. Their time on the Lakers together also produced the second-, fourth-, and seventh-highest duo performances.

MENTORING A-ROD

Coaching a sport involves much more than the mechanics and secrets of succeeding at any particular game. It's mostly mental: helping players get into the right headspace with focus, confidence, calm, and resolve. Kobe Bryant possessed all those skills, and it informed his basketball playing to a level of iconic and statistical greatness. He also shared his general motivational techniques and tactics with world-class athletes in other sports, notably Alex Rodriguez, the heavily decorated athlete for baseball's New York Yankees.

Rodriguez and Bryant met as teenagers in the 1990s, entering and then dominating their respective sports around the same time. They stayed friends and colleagues for years, with Kobe pushing a sometimes-faltering Rodriguez to achieve great things. "His work ethic was impeccable, and his stress on mastering the fundamentals is what elevated him to the player he was," Rodriguez said. "He followed my career and would often call to help with my health, daily routines, and would even chime in about hitting techniques." Thanks to Kobe's assistance, A-Rod was as accomplished as the Mamba, with fourteen All-Star game appearances, three Most Valuable Player awards, and a World Series championship.

★ **FACT** ★

In the **1996** NBA Draft, high school senior Kobe Bryant was selected **13TH** by the Charlotte Hornets, who immediately traded him to the Los Angeles Lakers in exchange for veteran center Vlade Divac.

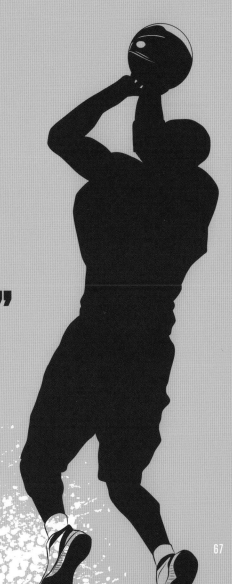

"IF YOU LOVE THE GAME, THEN YOU'VE ALREADY WON."

ELEVATING
WOMEN'S BASKETBALL

Kobe Bryant was a widely admired sports figure, and he often used his influence to promote not himself and his team but to respectfully raise awareness of women's basketball. The WNBA launched around the same time that Kobe began his NBA career, and it became the longest-lasting and most viable professional women's sports league in American history. Kobe was a staunch advocate for women's basketball, publicly elevating the stature of the WNBA and promoting women's basketball in general, which was traditionally overlooked by the general public and sports media. Kobe's eldest daughter, Gianna, was a basketball prodigy, and he personally mentored and coached her and her youth teams, and the pair were often spotted courtside at games.

Kobe was a personal hero, aspirational figure, and inspirational guide for Candace Parker, the most celebrated WNBA player of the twenty-first century. Parker was close with the Bryant family, and when she led her team, the Chicago Sky, to a league title in 2021 (a year after the deaths of Kobe and Gianna), the deceased pair were in her thoughts. "I think Kobe and Gigi have meant so much to our league," Parker said. "The advice I got from Vanessa [Bryant, Kobe's wife] before the game was, 'Play Gigi's way.' And I think we've done that."

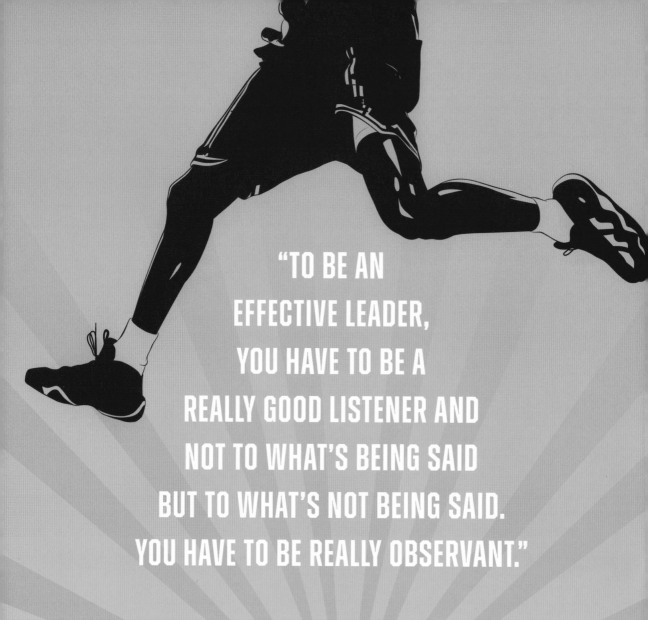

"TO BE AN
EFFECTIVE LEADER,
YOU HAVE TO BE A
REALLY GOOD LISTENER AND
NOT TO WHAT'S BEING SAID
BUT TO WHAT'S NOT BEING SAID.
YOU HAVE TO BE REALLY OBSERVANT."

KOBE!

Kobe scored more than 40 POINTS in a game 122 TIMES, more than 50 POINTS 25 TIMES, more than 60 POINTS SIX TIMES, and he scored the SECOND-MOST POINTS ever in a game, with an 81-POINT PERFORMANCE in 2006.

THAT'S *SO* MAMBA

KOBE WASN'T JUST A TOP SCORER—HE SET UP SUCCESSFUL PLAYS FOR HIS TEAMMATES, TOO. IN 2014, KOBE BRYANT BECAME THE FIRST PLAYER IN NBA HISTORY TO RECORD

MORE THAN 30,000 POINTS ALONG WITH 6,000 ASSISTS.

GO, KOBE, *GO!*

Kobe Bryant was selected to **18** NBA ALL-STAR TEAMS, including 17 in a row.

DID *YOU* KNOW?

Kobe is the only Naismith Memorial Basketball Hall of Fame member to also win an Academy Award. In 2018, he won Best Animated Short Film for *Dear Basketball.*

KOBE BEING KOBE

Kobe Bryant is the Los Angeles Lakers'

ALL-TIME LEADER

in games played, minutes played, points scored, shots both attempted and made, three-pointers attempted and made, and free throws attempted and made.

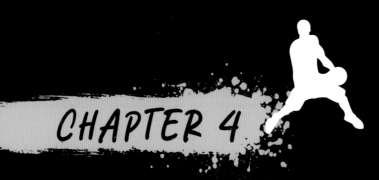

CHAPTER 4

THE INNOVATOR

Kobe Bryant's innate drive wasn't applicable only to basketball. His zest and quest to win also manifested as an insatiable curiosity and a desire to try things beyond sports. Both during and after his active playing career, Kobe launched ambitious ventures in business, the arts, education, and charity. Why? He had an active mind and realized that there was a lot more to life than playing basketball. Kobe possessed the influence, connections, and skills to give back to the community and change the lives of others, all while carving out new and interesting paths for himself. Making an effort and giving it everything you've got—that's just another part of Kobe's "Mamba Mentality," after all.

MOVING TO
THE MOVIES

Most NBA legends before him announced their retirement with a press release or a news conference. Kobe Bryant wrote a poem. "Dear Basketball" was an ode to the sport he loved and which loved him back. "I did everything for you / Because that's what you do / When someone makes you feel as / Alive as you've made me feel," Kobe wrote in part.

That poem, issued during Kobe's final season, would hint at how the world-class athlete would follow up his basketball career and where his ambitions and interests for the future would lie. Kobe formed Granity Studios, a multimedia production company through which the NBA great could further share, explain, and celebrate his deeply emotional and intellectual passion for basketball. With Granity Studios, Kobe produced and hosted *Detail*, a basketball analysis program that focused on one game or one player; the autobiographical documentary *Muse*; and *Dear Basketball*, an animated short film adaptation of his famous poem. The first short film he'd ever made, *Dear Basketball* won an Emmy Award for TV excellence, a Webby Award for online content, an Annie Award for superior animation work, and an Academy Award for Best Animated Short Subject.

75

"DEDICATION MAKES DREAMS COME TRUE."

★ FACT ★

Braveheart and *Dear Basketball*
are the only adaptations
of poems to ever win a

"BEST FILM"

Academy Award.

IT'S GOT TO
BE THE SHOES

Like many other basketball players who dazzled the NBA before, during, and after their tenures, Kobe Bryant landed a lucrative athletic shoe endorsement contract, specifically with industry leader Nike. Many players consider this a sign they have made the big time, and they proudly promote the shoes others design for them by wearing them on the court and starring in TV commercials. Kobe enjoyed those benefits and worked with shoemakers in such a manner, but he also took any shoe that bore his name very seriously.

During his career, athletic brands released twenty-two different Kobe-branded signature sneakers. Kobe took advantage of the shoe technology and development resources of firms like Nike to help design his ideal basketball sneaker. He constantly tweaked designs and came up with new ideas to give him an on-the-court advantage. For example, Kobe requested that for one release, Nike insert a special metal alloy band into the shoes' arches, because he believed it would shave off as much as a fraction of his reaction time when going for the ball. Then he had Nike create for him a shoe with an attached sock; he speculated that eliminating even the tiny amount of space between traditional sock and shoe would make his foot slide less and thus maximize his running speed.

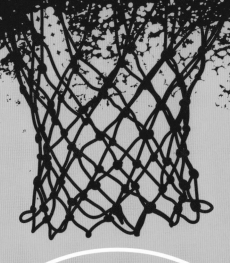

★ FACT ★

During his career, Kobe Bryant earned **$680** million. About **$323** million came from his player salary, and the rest came from endorsements, particularly his Nike deal.

"THESE YOUNG GUYS ARE PLAYING CHECKERS. I'M OUT THERE PLAYING CHESS."

MAMBA SCHOOL

In 2016, youth basketball coach Jon Spotts founded the Sports Academy, a training facility with two locations in southern California. Two years later, he recruited another coach he met on the circuit, Kobe Bryant, who was so excited about the possibilities of the Academy that he joined the business as a very active partner. Kobe allowed the program to be renamed after his court persona, thus creating the Mamba Sports Academy. Under the guidance of Kobe, the Mamba Sports Academy became one of the world's most prestigious, progressive, and state-of-the-art sports training facilities, using resources like science and technology to apply the NBA legend's principles and keys to athletic excellence.

The Mamba Sports Academy houses carefully designed and intricately executed training programs, a venture lab, physical therapy facilities, and high-tech sports simulations, all while hosting teams and tournaments in basketball and volleyball. "It's our physical space to actually help young athletes get better," Kobe said in 2019. "So we have the information, we have the inspiration, and now we actually have the facility where the rubber kind of meets the road, where athletes can come and train and actually do the work to get better mentally and physically."

"EVERYTHING I'M BUILDING NOW IS *BECAUSE OF THEM AND FOR THEM....* AS A COACH FOR ONE OF MY DAUGHTER'S TEAMS, I ALSO HOPE TO PASS ALONG A LITTLE BASKETBALL KNOWLEDGE TOO."

THE WIZENARD SERIES TRAINING CAMP

THE WIZENARD SERIES SEASON ONE

EPOCA THE TREE OF ECROF

EPOCA THE RIVER OF SAND

KOBE
BOOKS IT

After giving writing and arts a try with his basketball retirement poem "Dear Basketball" and the Oscar-winning adaptation, Kobe Bryant used much of the time that opened up after he left the Los Angeles Lakers on literary pursuits. In 2018, he reflected on the unique, all-in physical and mental approach he pioneered on the court in *The Mamba Mentality: How I Play*, a memoir of Kobe's basketball years but with insight toward the mental and philosophical approaches he developed that informed his playing and beyond.

A personal, informative book on basketball was just Kobe's literary warm-up. After *The Mamba Mentality*, Kobe created, developed, and published (via his media company) the *Wizenard* series of fantasy novels about a terrible youth basketball team that gets better with incredible effort, hard work, trust in one another, and the guidance of a wise coach with magical powers. Kobe enjoyed creation so much that he also shepherded *Epoca*, a sports-fantasy series about a magical athletic academy.

DID YOU KNOW?

The Kobe and Vanessa Bryant Family Foundation helped fund COACH for Kids and Their Families. **A MOBILE MEDICAL ORGANIZATION** benefiting underserved and poorly resourced Los Angeles neighborhoods.

THAT'S SO MAMBA

KOBE BRYANT WAS ONE OF THE CHIEF INVESTORS IN THE NATIONAL MUSEUM OF AFRICAN AMERICAN HISTORY AND CULTURE, DONATING **$1 MILLION** TO OPEN THE SMITHSONIAN OFFSHOOT.

BE MORE KOBE

KOBE BRYANT WAS AMONG THE MAKE-A-WISH FOUNDATION'S MOST REQUESTED AND PROLIFIC PARTICIPANTS. OVER 20 YEARS, HE MET WITH MORE THAN 100 CHILDREN GRAPPLING WITH SERIOUS OR LIFE-THREATENING ILLNESSES.

KOBE!

Through his involvement with Stand Up to Cancer, Kobe raised **$81 MILLION FOR CANCER** research in 2012 alone.

THE KOBE WAY

CHARITABLE AFTER DEATH: In 2022, Vanessa Bryant donated the $16 million settlement from a lawsuit over the illegal distribution of photos of the crash that killed Kobe Bryant to the Mamba and Mambacita Sports Foundation, a charity the basketball legend founded.

"USE YOUR SUCCESS, WEALTH, AND INFLUENCE TO PUT THEM IN THE BEST POSITION TO REALIZE THEIR OWN DREAMS AND FIND THEIR TRUE PURPOSE."

KOBE GIVES BACK

In his two decades as a dominant, popular, title-winning, and praise-collecting NBA superstar, Kobe Bryant acquired a lot of money, a lot of influence, and the support of some very important people. After just a few years in the league, he'd amassed a fortune as well as a clarity of what to do with all the money. Kobe wanted to help others in very specific ways, so that's what he set out to do.

In 2006, Kobe and his wife started what would evolve into The Kobe and Vanessa Bryant Family Foundation. It funds educational, social, and sports programs for economically disadvantaged kids and families. The charity has awarded countless scholarships to potential college students of color from lower-income backgrounds and also pushes resources to the Make-A-Wish Foundation. In tandem with another organization he helped create, the Kobe Bryant China Fund, Kobe's Family Foundation runs cultural exchange programs between the United States and China for middle school students. The goal: create "life-changing experiences designed to broaden their global perspectives." Kobe also devoted much of his time to other charities, such as After-School All-Stars, a nonprofit that runs afternoon programs in twelve cities for low-income kids.

CHAPTER 5

THE COMEBACK KING

When times are tough, it takes real mettle, inner strength, confidence, and sheer will to win—or to even *try* to win. Kobe Bryant has gone down in history as one of basketball's greatest champions, a five-time title winner, and an NBA Most Valuable Player, but like nearly all high-level athletes who play professional sports, Kobe Bryant suffered numerous setbacks and disappointments. Some of these blows included potentially career-ending injuries and humiliating losses that came despite his best efforts at preparation and rising to every challenge that came his way. Failure is a part of life, and it's a part of sports, but the people who are remembered—those exemplary figures among us—are those who can rise up from disappointment, put behind them what is keeping them down, and succeed again. Here are some times when Kobe Bryant proved himself to be the master of the comeback. Kobe was a player who came through in the clutch for his teammates. He frequently became a late-game hero, providing exhilarating, and almost impossible come-from-behind victories. These are some of Kobe's best-ever games and moments.

ACHILLES HEEL

On April 12, 2013, Kobe Bryant and the Lakers played in their 80th game of the 82-game NBA regular season. The team was in the midst of a winning streak to secure a playoff spot, with Kobe scoring thirty and forty-seven points in the 81st and 82nd game and thirty-four in the 80th game—despite hyperextending his left knee in the third quarter. With three minutes to go in the game, Kobe tried maneuvering around Harrison Barnes, a normal move that went wrong as he was fouled and then heard an audible pop before collapsing to the floor and clutching his left ankle. Kobe immediately knew he'd torn his Achilles tendon. He hobbled to the key, landed his free throws, and exited the game (which the Lakers won by two points).

Tests showed that Kobe had endured a third-degree tear in the Achilles, the thickest tendon in the body and one that makes running and jumping possible. He'd be out of the sport that requires those skills—indefinitely. The vast majority of players who had torn their Achilles had never even returned to play, and those who had returned played at a significantly diminished level. Following surgery, six weeks of rehabilitation, and then a slow recovery process, Kobe was able to practice basketball again in mid-November 2013. Just weeks later, on December 8, Kobe Bryant suited up for the Lakers and played in the starting lineup. The Lakers lost to the Toronto Raptors, but Kobe, in limited minutes, scored nine points, pulled down eight rebounds, and accumulated four assists. The Mamba was back.

"NO MATTER WHAT THE INJURY—UNLESS IT'S COMPLETELY DEBILITATING— I'M GOING TO BE THE SAME PLAYER I'VE ALWAYS BEEN. I'LL FIGURE IT OUT. I'LL MAKE SOME TWEAKS, SOME CHANGES, BUT I'M STILL COMING."

★ FACT ★

You can't make the shots you don't take, but even the greats don't always succeed. Kobe Bryant, for example, is the NBA's all-time leader in missed shots, with **14,481**.

RETURN FROM A
TORN KNEE MUSCLE

Kobe Bryant's post-Achilles tendon rupture comeback early in the 2013–2014 season wouldn't last. Just eleven days after he entered the Los Angeles Lakers roster late due to one major injury, he suffered another setback. During a game against the Memphis Grizzlies, Kobe tried to double back on a play, ran right up against a defender, and then fell onto his left knee. He twisted it but kept playing, reporting after the game that his knee felt stiff. A doctor's examination would reveal that Kobe hadn't just sprained or overextended the knee—he'd fractured the lateral tibial plateau. The Lakers' medics initially speculated that Kobe would miss six weeks' worth of games. Instead, he missed the entire rest of the 2013–2014 season.

After nearly a year of rest, recovery, and rehabilitation, Kobe was able to play again, and he was as good as he'd always been, if not better. In the Lakers' first twenty-five games of the season, Kobe led the scoring drive in nineteen, and then he passed Michael Jordan for third place on the NBA's all-time scoring list.

"IF I FAIL TODAY, I'M GOING TO *LEARN SOMETHING FROM THAT FAILURE.* I'M GOING TO TRY AGAIN."

A COMEBACK IN
THE 2000 WESTERN CONFERENCE FINALS

Despite boasting two of the league's top scorers of the year in Shaquille O'Neal and Kobe Bryant and amassing a by-far league best record of sixty-seven and fifteen, the Los Angeles Lakers found themselves in the decisive Game 7 of a grueling Western Conference Finals against their frequent playoff opponents, the underdog Portland Trail Blazers. After three quarters, the Blazers led 71 to 58, a seemingly insurmountable lead, almost guaranteeing a trip to the NBA Finals for Portland.

But Kobe Bryant thrived under pressure, coming alive where other players may have buckled or crumbled. He led an improbable and unstoppable fourth-quarter comeback, with the Lakers scoring thirty-one points. Of those, eleven were from Kobe, while the entire Portland squad could only come up with thirteen. In the end, Kobe led the Lakers in points (twenty-five) *and* rebounds (eleven) and assists (seven). With Kobe leading the way and getting the job done, the Lakers won the game by five points and thus the series, with Kobe punching his ticket to his first NBA Finals.

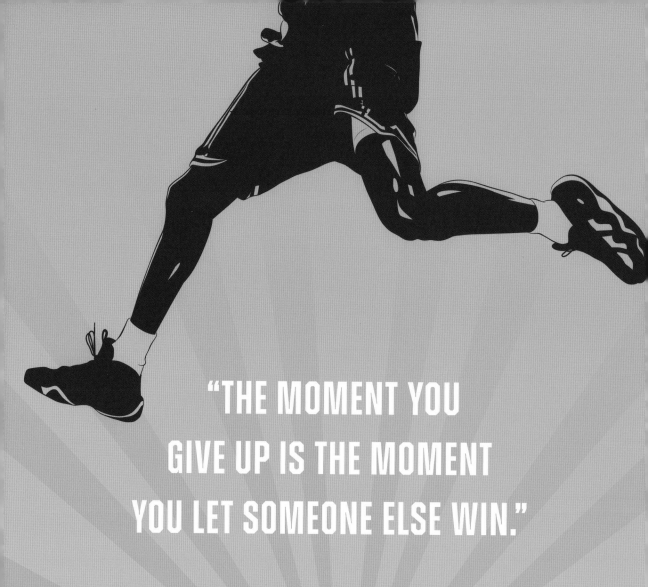

"THE MOMENT YOU
GIVE UP IS THE MOMENT
YOU LET SOMEONE ELSE WIN."

★ FACT ★

Kobe engineered fourth-quarter comebacks in the regular season too. In a 2002 game against the Dallas Mavericks, the Lakers trailed by **27 POINTS** going into the final frame but won **105** to **103**, thanks to 21 late points from Kobe.

A COMEBACK IN
THE 2002 WESTERN CONFERENCE FINALS

The 2002 NBA Western Conference Finals stretched out to the full seven games. The Los Angeles Lakers faced the Sacramento Kings, and Kobe Bryant put on one of the all-time most spectacular sustained efforts in playoff history, averaging 27.1 points, 6.3 rebounds, and 3.9 assists. All that consistency over the series almost wasn't enough—Kobe would have to dig deep to find the strength and calm under pressure, to pull out all the stops, and make sure his Lakers represented the West in NBA Finals for the third consecutive year.

The Lakers and Kings won Games 4 and 5, respectively, each by one point, after which Sacramento held a three to two series lead, with only one more victory necessary to reach the Finals. The Lakers eked out a Game 6 win, forcing a deciding seventh game, which featured nineteen lead changes and sixteen ties—including the one at the end of regulation, forcing overtime. Bryant hit the bench for less than a minute for the whole game, continuously playing and amassing thirty points, ten rebounds, and seven assists. But when it was all said and done, the underdog Lakers defeated the #1 seeded Sacramento Kings by six points.

★ FACT ★

Kobe was named the NBA's player of the month **17 TIMES** and player of the week **33 TIMES**—the equivalent of 2 full seasons and 1 whole season, respectively.

"EVERYTHING NEGATIVE— PRESSURE, CHALLENGES— IS ALL AN OPPORTUNITY FOR ME TO RISE."

THE LAST BEST
GAME OF ALL TIME

Sometimes a comeback doesn't have to result in a victory. There can be a personal win embedded within, and there's something admirable about finishing strong, because that's still a triumph over adversity as well as a powerful final act. Kobe Bryant announced in November 2015 that the 2015–2016 NBA season would be his last, his twentieth season total in a career spent entirely with the Los Angeles Lakers. It was as good a time as any for Kobe to retire—almost nobody plays professional basketball for as long as he did, and toward the end, his stats suffered and lingering injury issues caught up to him. In his final game, Kobe provided a glimpse of his glory days, a last reminder to the world, his fans, and himself of why he was considered one of the greatest and most dynamic players ever to lace up a pair of sneakers.

On April 13, 2016, the Lakers played the Utah Jazz in a meaningless game, as both teams had already been eliminated from a playoff spot. The attention and historical spotlight were both on Kobe, who performed well in the first half, scoring twenty-two points. After halftime, and with the end of his storied career in sight, Kobe ignited, scoring fifteen points in the third quarter and twenty-three in the fourth quarter. Kobe scored the Lakers' final fifteen points in the final three minutes, turning around a 94 to 84 deficit into a 101 to 96 final score. Kobe won his last game, and he set a record for most points in a last game: sixty.

KOBE!

8

Kobe came into the NBA wearing a number 8 on his jersey, as he'd done as a youth basketball player. He wanted to wear another number he liked, 24, but it was in use. When it became available in 2006, Kobe switched to number 24. Upon his retirement, the Lakers retired both numbers, making him the only player in NBA history to have his jersey retired twice.

THE **KOBE** WAY

Kobe almost always appeared on some kind of season-end "best of" list. He was named to 15 ALL-NBA TEAMS and 12 ALL-DEFENSIVE TEAMS and was named the NBA'S MVP IN 2008.

THAT'S *SO* MAMBA

KOBE TOOK **50 SHOTS** *DURING HIS LAST GAME, THE MOST SHOTS IN A GAME BY AN INDIVIDUAL IN NBA HISTORY.*

BE *MORE* KOBE

KOBE HAD 4 ASSISTS IN HIS FINAL GAME, INCLUDING ON HIS LAST-EVER PLAY— JORDAN CLARKSON SCORED AFTER KOBE LAUNCHED A FULL-COURT PASS HIS WAY.

DID *YOU* KNOW?

Kobe later claimed to be extremely nervous before his last game, which is why he missed his first 5 shots of the night.

GO, KOBE, *GO!*

With **60 POINTS** in his last contest, 37-year-old Kobe became **THE OLDEST PLAYER** to score that many points in an NBA game.

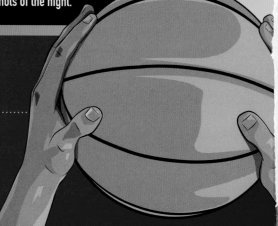